Book & CD for B♭, E♭, Bass Clef and C instruments

VOLUME
3

PLAY 8 SONGS WITH A PROFESSIONAL BAND

HOW TO USE THE CD:

Each song has <u>two</u> tracks:

1) Full Stereo Mix

All recorded instruments are present on this track.

2) Split Track

Piano and **Bass** parts can be removed
by turning down the volume on the LEFT channel.

Guitar and **Harmonica** parts can be removed
by turning down the volume on the RIGHT channel.

ISBN 978-1-4234-5349-9

7777 W. BLUEMOUND RD. P.O. BOX 13819 MILWAUKEE, WI 53213

Visit Hal Leonard Online at
www.halleonard.com

SLOW BLUES

3. Well, __ some - day ba - by,

ba - by, when you change your __ mind.

yeah, __ some - day ba - by,

ba - by, when you change your _____ mind, __

no, __ you won't have to search the whole world __ o - ver,

'cause I won't __ be hard to find. _____

Additional Lyrics

2. Hey baby, I don't like what you been puttin' down.
Hey baby, I don't like what you been puttin' down.
Oh, I'd search the whole world over,
Another love like yours can't be found.

Five Long Years

Words and Music by Eddie Boyd

1. Have you ev-er been mis-treat - ed?
2. See additional lyrics

You know _____ just what I'm talk-in' a-

bout.

Have you ev-er been mis-treat - ed?

You know _____ just what I'm talk-in' a-

bout.

I worked five ___ long ___ years for ___

one wom - an. She had the nerve _____ to

Guitar Solo

PUT ME OUT.

TO PUT ME OUT.

Verse

3. I've fin-'lly learned my les -

- son, should 'a' long time a-go. ___ The next wom-an that I mar - ry, she gon-na

work and bring me the gold. _____ Have you ev-er been mis-treat - ed? ___

You know _____ just what I'm talk-in' a - bout. __

I worked five ___ long ___ years for one wom-an. ___

Freely

She had the nerve, she had the nerve, she had the nerve,

A tempo

She had the nerve _____ to put me out.

Additional Lyrics

2. I got a job in a steel mill, shuckin' steel like a slave.
Five long years ev'ry Friday I come straight home with all my pay.
Have you ever been mistreated? You know just what I'm talkin' about.
I worked five long years for one woman. She had the nerve to put me out.

7

I Can't Quit You Baby

Written by Willie Dixon

VERSE %

Slow shuffle ♩. = 62

1. Well, _____ I can't quit you, ba — by,

3. See additional lyrics

But I _____ got to put you down _ for a while. _____

Well, _ you know _____ I can't quit you, ba — by,

But I _____ got to put you down _ for a while. _____

Well, _ you messed up my hap-py home, babe, _____

Made _ me mis-treat _ my on-ly child. _____

Additional Lyrics

3. Well, I'm so tired I could cry.
I could just lay down and die.
Well, I'm so tired I could cry.
Ooh, I could just lay down and die.
Yes, you know you're the only one, darlin',
Ooh, you know you're my desire.

4. When you hear me moanin' and groanin', baby,
You know it hurts me way down inside.
Oh, when you hear me moanin' and groanin', baby,
Oh, you know it hurts me way down inside.
Oh, when you hear me holler, baby,
Ooh, you know you're my desire.

I Just Want to Make Love to You

Written by Willie Dixon

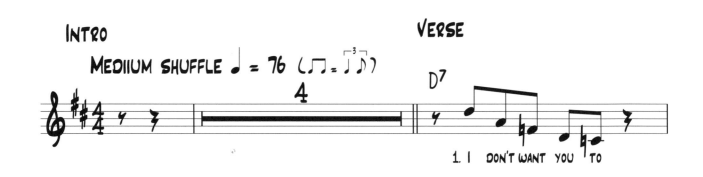

LOVE TO YOU, LOVE TO YOU, LOVE TO YOU.

HARP SOLO
D⁷

PLAY 11 TIMES

BRIDGE
G⁷

TELL BY THE WAY YOU SWISH AND WALK. I CAN SEE BY THE WAY YOU

BA - BY TALK. I CAN KNOW BY THE WAY YOU TREAT YOUR MAN THAT I COULD

A⁷ **VERSE** D⁷

LOVE YOU, __ BABE, UN - TIL THE CRY - IN' SHAME. 3. I DON'T WANT YOU

COOK MY BREAD. I DON'T WANT YOU TO MAKE MY BED.

I DON'T WANT __ YOU BE - CAUSE I'M SAD AND BLUE. __

REPEAT AND FADE

I JUST WANT TO MAKE LOVE TO YOU, LOVE TO YOU.

THE SKY IS CRYING
WORDS AND MUSIC BY ELMORE JAMES

VERSE

3. I've got a real, real, real, real bad feel-in' ___ that my ba-by, she don't ___ love me no more. ___

I've got a ___ real, real bad feel - in' that my ba - by don't ___ love me no more.

You know the sky, the sky's been cry-in', yeah.

Can you see the tears ___ roll down my nose?

RIT.

ADDITIONAL LYRICS

2. I saw my baby early one mornin',
   She was walkin' on down the street.
   I saw my baby early this mornin',
   She was walkin' on down the street.
   You know it hurt me, hurt me so bad,
   Made my poor heart, uh, skip a beat.

(They Call It)
Stormy Monday
(Stormy Monday Blues)
Words and Music by Aaron "T-Bone" Walker

Intro

Slow shuffle ♩. = 66

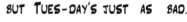

Verse

1. They call it storm-y Mon-day, but Tues-day's just as bad.
2. See additional lyrics

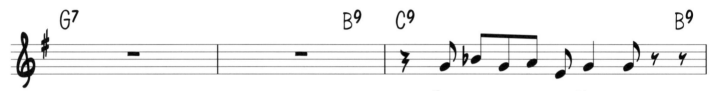

They call it storm-y Mon-day,

but Tues-day's just as bad. ____

Wednes-day's worse. ___ and ___ Thurs-day's al-so sad. ___

2. Yes. ____

ADDITIONAL LYRICS

2. Yes, the eagle flies on Friday, and Saturday I go out to play.
Eagle flies on Friday, and Saturday I go out to play.
Sunday I go to church, then I kneel down and pray.

Sweet Little Angel

Words and Music by B.B. King and Jules Bihari

ADDITIONAL LYRICS

2. I asked my baby for a nickel
   And she gave me a twenty dollar bill.
   Yes, asked my baby for a nickel
   And she gave me a twenty dollar bill.
   Yes, you know I asked her for a little drink o' liquor,
   And she gave me a whiskey still.

CD TRACK

8 Full Stereo Mix

16 Split Mix

C Version

Texas Flood

Words and Music by Larry Davis and Joseph W. Scott

Additional Lyrics

2. Well, dark clouds are rollin'.
   Man, I'm standin' out in the rain. Mm.
   Dark clouds are rollin'.
   Man, I'm standin' out in the rain.
   Well, flood waters keeps on rollin'.
   Man, it's about to drive me insane. Mm.

Don't Throw Your Love on Me So Strong

Words and Music by Albert King

Additional Lyrics

2. Hey baby, I don't like what you been puttin' down.
Hey baby, I don't like what you been puttin' down.
Oh, I'd search the whole world over,
Another love like yours can't be found.

Five Long Years

Words and Music by Eddie Boyd

Intro

Slow shuffle ♩. = 66

Verse

1. Have you ev-er been mis-treat - ed? _
2. See additional lyrics

You know _____ just what I'm talk-in' a-

bout. Have you ev-er been mis-treat -

- ED? You know _____ just what I'm talk-in' a-

bout. I worked five ___ long ___ years for ___

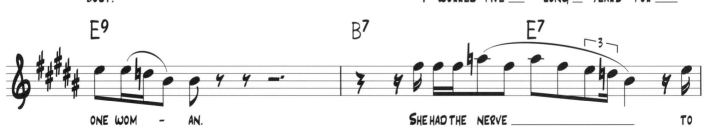

one wom - an. She had the nerve _____ to

I Can't Quit You Baby

Written by Willie Dixon

Additional Lyrics

3. Well, I'm so tired I could cry.
    I could just lay down and die.
    Well, I'm so tired I could cry.
    Ooh, I could just lay down and die.
    Yes, you know you're the only one, darlin',
    Ooh, you know you're my desire.

4. When you hear me moanin' and groanin', baby,
    You know it hurts me way down inside.
    Oh, when you hear me moanin' and groanin', baby,
    Oh, you know it hurts me way down inside.
    Oh, when you hear me holler, baby,
    Ooh, you know you're my desire.

I Just Want to Make Love to You

Written by Willie Dixon

INTRO

Medium shuffle ♩ = 76

VERSE

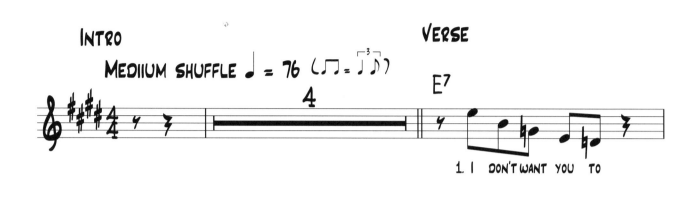

26

LOVE TO YOU. LOVE TO YOU. LOVE TO YOU.

HARP SOLO

E7

Play 11 times

BRIDGE

A7

TELL BY THE WAY YOU SWISH AND WALK. I CAN SEE BY THE WAY YOU

BA-BY TALK. I CAN KNOW BY THE WAY YOU TREAT YOUR MAN THAT I COULD

VERSE

B7

E7

LOVE YOU, __ BABE, UN-TIL THE CRY-IN' SHAME. 3. I DON'T WANT YOU

COOK MY BREAD. I DON'T WANT YOU TO MAKE MY BED.

I DON'T WANT __ YOU BE-CAUSE I'M SAD AND BLUE. __

Repeat and fade

I JUST WANT TO MAKE LOVE TO YOU, LOVE TO YOU.

The Sky Is Crying

Words and Music by Elmore James

ADDITIONAL LYRICS

2. I saw my baby early one mornin',
   She was walkin' on down the street.
   I saw my baby early this mornin',
   She was walkin' on down the street.
   You know it hurt me, hurt me so bad,
   Made my poor heart, uh, skip a beat.

(They Call It)
STORMY MONDAY
(Stormy Monday Blues)
Words and Music by Aaron "T-Bone" Walker

INTRO

SLOW SHUFFLE ♩. = 66

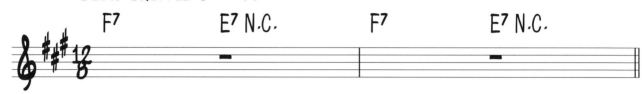

VERSE

1. They call it storm-y Mon-day, but Tues-day's just as bad.
2. See additional lyrics

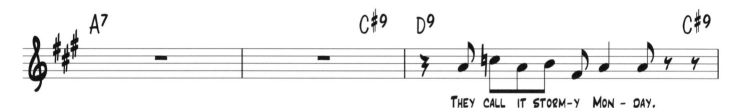

They call it storm-y Mon-day,

but Tues day's just as bad. ___

Wednes-day's worse. ___ and ___ Thurs-day's al-so sad. ___

2. Yes. ___

ADDITIONAL LYRICS

2. YES, THE EAGLE FLIES ON FRIDAY, AND SATURDAY I GO OUT TO PLAY.
EAGLE FLIES ON FRIDAY, AND SATURDAY I GO OUT TO PLAY.
SUNDAY I GO TO CHURCH, THEN I KNEEL DOWN AND PRAY.

Sweet Little Angel

Words and Music by B.B. King and Jules Bihari

Intro

Slow shuffle ♩. = 64

Additional Lyrics

2. I asked my baby for a nickel
   And she gave me a twenty dollar bill.
   Yes, asked my baby for a nickel
   And she gave me a twenty dollar bill.
   Yes, you know I asked her for a little drink o' liquor,
   And she gave me a whiskey still.

Texas Flood

Words and Music by Larry Davis and Joseph W. Scott

Intro
Slow shuffle ♩. = 68

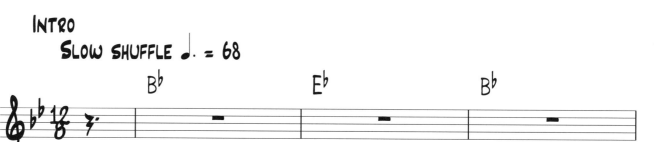

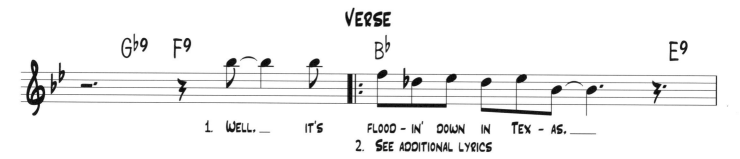

1. Well,___ it's flood-in' down in Tex-as,___
2. See additional lyrics

and all ___ the tel-e-phone lines ___ are down.   Well,___ it's

flood-in' down _ in Tex-as,   and all ___ the tel-e-phone lines _____ are

down.   Well, I been try -

- in' to call _ my ba-by, _____   but _ I can't get a sin - gle sound. _

Additional Lyrics

2. Well, dark clouds are rollin'.
   Man, I'm standin' out in the rain. Mm.
   Dark clouds are rollin'.
   Man, I'm standin' out in the rain.
   Well, flood waters keeps on rollin'.
   Man, it's about to drive me insane. Mm.

1. Full Stereo Mix
9. Split Mix

Eb Version

Don't Throw Your Love on Me So Strong

Words and Music by Albert King

'CAUSE I WON'T _ BE HARD TO FIND. _____

ADDITIONAL LYRICS

2. HEY BABY, I DON'T LIKE WHAT YOU BEEN PUTTIN' DOWN.
   HEY BABY, I DON'T LIKE WHAT YOU BEEN PUTTIN' DOWN.
   OH, I'D SEARCH THE WHOLE WORLD OVER,
   ANOTHER LOVE LIKE YOURS CAN'T BE FOUND.

Five Long Years
Words and Music by Eddie Boyd

Intro
Slow shuffle ♩. = 66

1. Have you ev-er been mis-treat - ed? _
2. See additional lyrics

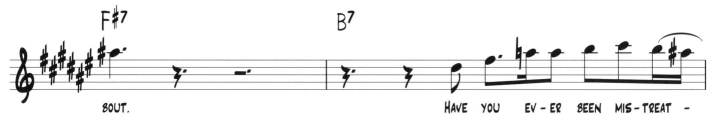

You know _____ just what I'm talk-in' a-

bout.   Have you ev-er been mis-treat -

- ed?   You know _____ just what I'm talk-in' a-

bout.   I worked five __ long __ years for __

one wom - an.   She had the nerve _____ to

GUITAR SOLO

PUT ME OUT.   TO PUT ME OUT.

VERSE

3. I'VE FIN-'LLY LEARNED MY LES -

- SON.   SHOULD 'A' LONGTIME A-GO. __   THE NEXT WOM AN THAT I MAR - RY. SHE GON-NA

WORK AND BRING ME THE GOLD. _____   HAVE YOU EV-ER BEEN MIS-TREAT - ED? __

YOU KNOW _____ JUST WHAT I'M TALK IN' A - BOUT. __

I WORKED FIVE __ LONG __ YEARS FOR ONE WOM AN. ____

FREELY

SHE HAD THE NERVE.   SHE HAD THE NERVE.   SHE HAD THE NERVE.

A TEMPO

F#7 F#7/A# F#7/B F#7/B F#/C# G9 F#9

SHE HAD THE NERVE _____ TO PUT ME OUT.

ADDITIONAL LYRICS

2. I GOT A JOB IN A STEEL MILL, SHUCKIN' STEEL LIKE A SLAVE.
FIVE LONG YEARS EV'RY FRIDAY I COME STRAIGHT HOME WITH ALL MY PAY.
HAVE YOU EVER BEEN MISTREATED? YOU KNOW JUST WHAT I'M TALKIN' ABOUT.
I WORKED FIVE LONG YEARS FOR ONE WOMAN. SHE HAD THE NERVE TO PUT ME OUT.

I Can't Quit You Baby

Written by Willie Dixon

Additional Lyrics

3. WELL, I'M SO TIRED I COULD CRY.
    I COULD JUST LAY DOWN AND DIE.
    WELL, I'M SO TIRED I COULD CRY.
    OOH, I COULD JUST LAY DOWN AND DIE.
    YES, YOU KNOW YOU'RE THE ONLY ONE, DARLIN',
    OOH, YOU KNOW YOU'RE MY DESIRE.

4. WHEN YOU HEAR ME MOANIN' AND GROANIN', BABY,
    YOU KNOW IT HURTS ME WAY DOWN INSIDE.
    OH, WHEN YOU HEAR ME MOANIN' AND GROANIN', BABY,
    OH, YOU KNOW IT HURTS ME WAY DOWN INSIDE.
    OH, WHEN YOU HEAR ME HOLLER, BABY,
    OOH, YOU KNOW YOU'RE MY DESIRE.

I Just Want to Make Love to You

Written by Willie Dixon

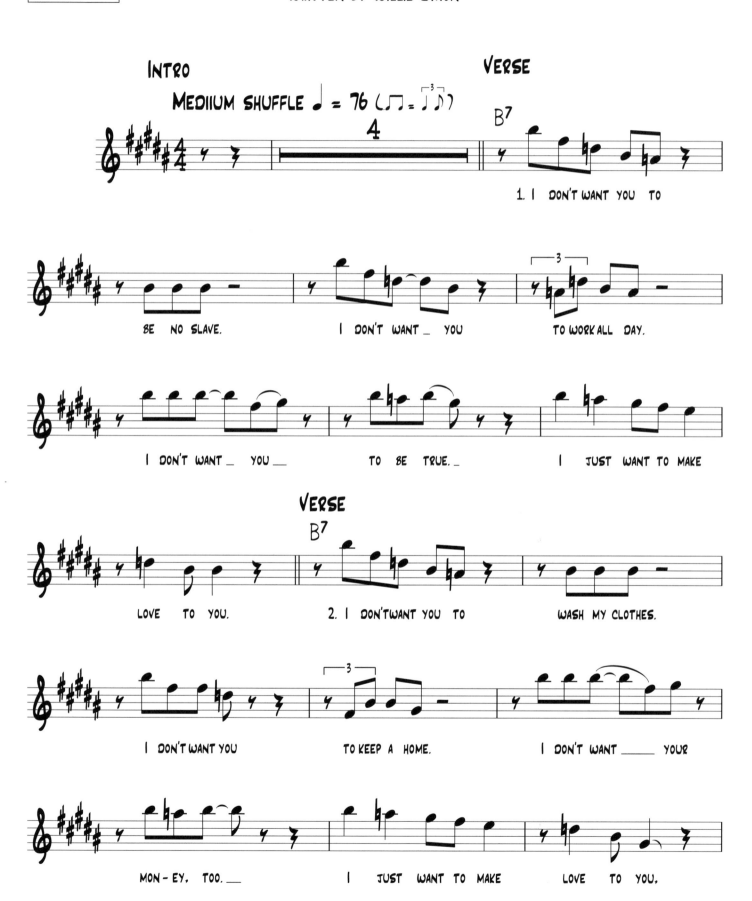

The Sky Is Crying

Words and Music by Elmore James

3. I'VE GOT A REAL, REAL, REAL, REAL BAD FEEL-IN' THAT MY BA-BY, SHE DON'T LOVE ME NO MORE. I'VE GOT A REAL, REAL BAD FEEL-IN' THAT MY BA-BY DON'T LOVE ME NO MORE. YOU KNOW THE SKY, THE SKY'S BEEN CRY-IN', YEAH. CAN YOU SEE THE TEARS ROLL DOWN MY NOSE?

ADDITIONAL LYRICS

2. I SAW MY BABY EARLY ONE MORNIN',
   SHE WAS WALKIN' ON DOWN THE STREET.
   I SAW MY BABY EARLY THIS MORNIN',
   SHE WAS WALKIN' ON DOWN THE STREET.
   YOU KNOW IT HURT ME, HURT ME SO BAD,
   MADE MY POOR HEART, UH, SKIP A BEAT.

(THEY CALL IT)
STORMY MONDAY
(STORMY MONDAY BLUES)
WORDS AND MUSIC BY AARON "T-BONE" WALKER

INTRO

SLOW SHUFFLE ♩. = 66

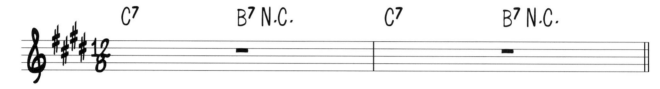

VERSE

1. They call it storm-y Mon-day,   but Tues-day's just as bad.
2. See additional lyrics

They call it storm-y Mon - day.

But Tues-day's just as bad. ____

Wednes-day's worse. _   and ___ Thurs-day's al - so sad. _

1. ____   2. Yes, _____

Additional Lyrics

2. Yes, the eagle flies on Friday, and Saturday I go out to play.
   Eagle flies on Friday, and Saturday I go out to play.
   Sunday I go to church, then I kneel down and pray.

Sweet Little Angel

Words and Music by B.B. King and Jules Bihari

Intro

Slow shuffle ♩. = 64

1. Got a sweet 'lil an-gel.
2. See additional lyrics

I love the way she spreads her wings.

Yes, got a sweet 'lil an - gel.

I love the way she spreads her wings.

Yes, when she spreads her wings a-round me,

I gets joy and ev-'ry-thing.

VERSE

MY BA - BY SHOULD QUIT ME, LORD. __ I DO BE - LIEVE __

__ I WOULD DIE. __ YES. __ IF MY BA - BY SHOULD QUIT ME.

LORD. __ I DO BE - LIEVE __ I WOULD DIE.

YES. __ IF YOU DON'T LOVE ME. LIT-TLE AN-GEL.

PLEASE __ TELL __ ME THE REA-SON WHY. __

ADDITIONAL LYRICS

2. I ASKED MY BABY FOR A NICKEL
   AND SHE GAVE ME A TWENTY DOLLAR BILL.
   YES, ASKED MY BABY FOR A NICKEL
   AND SHE GAVE ME A TWENTY DOLLAR BILL.
   YES, YOU KNOW I ASKED HER FOR A LITTLE DRINK O' LIQUOR,
   AND SHE GAVE ME A WHISKEY STILL.

Texas Flood

Words and Music by Larry Davis and Joseph W. Scott

Intro
Slow shuffle ♩. = 68

1. Well, __ it's flood-in' down in Tex-as, __
2. See additional lyrics

and all __ the tel-e-phone lines __ are down.   Well, __ it's

flood-in' down __ in Tex-as,   and all __ the tel-e-phone lines __ are

down.   Well, I been try-

-in' to call __ my ba-by, __   but __ I can't get a sin-gle sound. __

Additional Lyrics

2. Well, dark clouds are rollin'.
   Man, I'm standin' out in the rain. Mm.
   Dark clouds are rollin'.
   Man, I'm standin' out in the rain.
   Well, flood waters keeps on rollin'.
   Man, it's about to drive me insane. Mm.

Don't Throw Your Love on Me So Strong

Words and Music by Albert King

3. WELL,___ SOME - DAY BA - BY, BA - BY, WHEN YOU CHANGE YOUR ___ MIND.

YEAH,___ SOME - DAY BA - BY, BA - BY, WHEN YOU CHANGE YOUR _____ MIND, ___

NO,___ YOU WON'T HAVE TO SEARCH THE WHOLE WORLD_ O - VER,

'CAUSE I WON'T_ BE HARD TO FIND. _____

Additional Lyrics

2. Hey baby, I don't like what you been puttin' down.
Hey baby, I don't like what you been puttin' down.
Oh, I'd search the whole world over,
Another love like yours can't be found.

Five Long Years

Words and Music by Eddie Boyd

Intro
Slow shuffle ♩. = 66

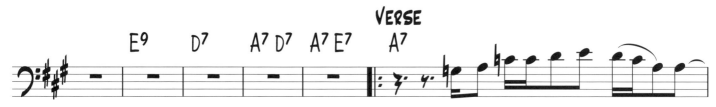

1. Have you ev-er been mis-treat - ed? _
2. See additional lyrics

You know _____ just what I'm talk - in' a -

bout. Have you ev - er been mis-treat -

- ed? You know _____ just what I'm talk - in' a -

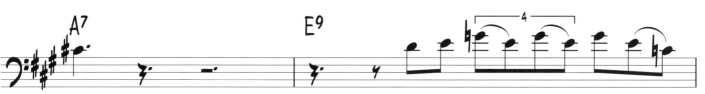

bout. I worked five ___ long ___ years for ___

one wom - an. She had the nerve _____ to

PUT ME OUT.

TO PUT ME OUT.

VERSE

3. I'VE FIN-'LLY LEARNED MY LES-

-SON. SHOULD 'A' LONG TIME A-GO.

THE NEXT WOM-AN THAT I MAR - RY, SHE GON-NA

WORK AND BRING ME THE GOLD.

HAVE YOU EV-ER BEEN MIS-TREAT - ED?

YOU KNOW JUST WHAT I'M TALK IN' A - BOUT.

I WORKED FIVE LONG YEARS FOR ONE WOM AN.

FREELY

SHE HAD THE NERVE,

SHE HAD THE NERVE,

SHE HAD THE NERVE,

A TEMPO

SHE HAD THE NERVE TO PUT ME OUT.

ADDITIONAL LYRICS

2. I GOT A JOB IN A STEEL MILL, SHUCKIN' STEEL LIKE A SLAVE.
FIVE LONG YEARS EV'RY FRIDAY I COME STRAIGHT HOME WITH ALL MY PAY.
HAVE YOU EVER BEEN MISTREATED? YOU KNOW JUST WHAT I'M TALKIN' ABOUT.
I WORKED FIVE LONG YEARS FOR ONE WOMAN. SHE HAD THE NERVE TO PUT ME OUT.

𝒥: C Version

I Can't Quit You Baby
Written by Willie Dixon

VERSE

SLOW SHUFFLE ♩. = 62

1. Well, _____ I can't quit you, ba - by,

3. See additional lyrics

But I _____ got to put you down _ for a while. _____

Well, _ you know _____ I can't quit you, ba - by,

But I _____ got to put you down _ for a while. _____

Well, _ you messed up my hap - py home, babe, _____

Made _ me mis - treat _____ my on - ly child. _____

VERSE

2. Yes,___ you know I love __ you, ba - by.
4. See additional lyrics

My love for you ____ I ____ could nev-er hide. _____

Well, _____ you know _____ I love you, ba - by.

My love for you ____ I ____ could nev-er hide. ____ Yes,_ you

To Coda ⊕

know I love you, ba - by. Well, _____ you just _____ my or - deredsize. _

D.S. al Coda

_____ 3. Well,___ I'm so _

Begin fade   **Fade out**

⊕ **Coda**

Ooh, ___ you know _____ you're _ my de-sire. ____

ADDITIONAL LYRICS

3. Well, I'm so tired I could cry.
   I could just lay down and die.
   Well, I'm so tired I could cry.
   Ooh, I could just lay down and die.
   Yes, you know you're the only one, darlin',
   Ooh, you know you're my desire.

4. When you hear me moanin' and groanin', baby,
   You know it hurts me way down inside.
   Oh, when you hear me moanin' and groanin', baby,
   Oh, you know it hurts me way down inside.
   Oh, when you hear me holler, baby,
   Ooh, you know you're my desire.

I Just Want to Make Love to You

Written by Willie Dixon

CD TRACK

4 Full Stereo Mix

12 Split Mix

C Version

LOVE TO YOU, LOVE TO YOU, LOVE TO YOU.

HARP SOLO
D7

Play 11 times

BRIDGE
G7

TELL BY THE WAY YOU SWISH AND WALK. I CAN SEE BY THE WAY YOU

BA-BY TALK. I CAN KNOW BY THE WAY YOU TREAT YOUR MAN THAT I COULD

A7   **VERSE**
D7

LOVE YOU,__ BABE, UN-TIL THE CRY-IN' SHAME. 3. I DON'T WANT YOU

COOK MY BREAD. I DON'T WANT YOU TO MAKE MY BED.

I DON'T WANT__ YOU BE-CAUSE I'M SAD AND BLUE.__

Repeat and fade

I JUST WANT TO MAKE LOVE TO YOU, LOVE TO YOU.

The Sky Is Crying

Words and Music by Elmore James

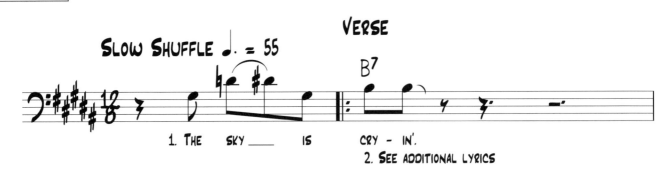

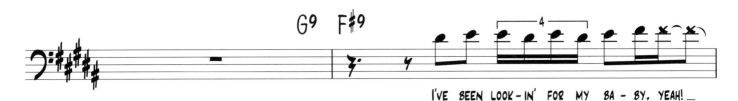

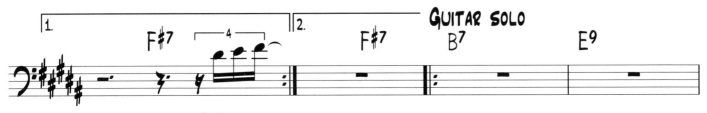

VERSE

3. I've got a real, real, real, real bad feel-in' ____ that my ba-by, she don't ____ love me no more. ____

I've got a ____ real, real bad feel-in' that my ba-by don't ____ love me no more.

You know the sky, the sky's been cry-in', yeah.

Can you see the tears ____ roll down my nose?

ADDITIONAL LYRICS

2. I saw my baby early one mornin',
   She was walkin' on down the street.
   I saw my baby early this mornin',
   She was walkin' on down the street.
   You know it hurt me, hurt me so bad,
   Made my poor heart, uh, skip a beat.

(They Call It)
STORMY MONDAY
(Stormy Monday Blues)
Words and Music by Aaron "T-Bone" Walker

INTRO

Slow shuffle ♩. = 66

VERSE

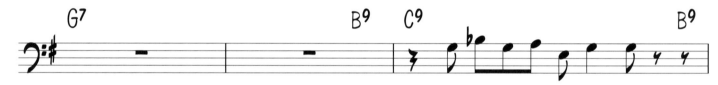

1. They call it storm-y Mon-day, but Tues-day's just as bad.
2. See additional lyrics

They call it storm-y Mon - day,

But Tues-day's just as bad. ___

Wednes-day's worse. ___ and ___ Thurs-day's al - so sad. ___

___ 2. Yes, _____

Additional Lyrics

2. Yes, the eagle flies on Friday, and Saturday I go out to play.
   Eagle flies on Friday, and Saturday I go out to play.
   Sunday I go to church, then I kneel down and pray.

𝄢 C Version

Sweet Little Angel
Words and Music by B.B. King and Jules Bihari

Intro

Slow shuffle ♩. = 64

Verse

1. Got a sweet 'lil an - gel.
2. See additional lyrics

I ___ love the way ___ she spreads ___ her wings. ___

Yes, ___ got a sweet 'lil an - gel.

I ___ love the way ___ she spreads her wings. ___

Yes, ___ when she spreads her wings ___ a-round me. ___

I gets joy ___ and ev-'ry-thing.

Additional Lyrics

2. I asked my baby for a nickel
   And she gave me a twenty dollar bill.
   Yes, asked my baby for a nickel
   And she gave me a twenty dollar bill.
   Yes, you know I asked her for a little drink o' liquor,
   And she gave me a whiskey still.

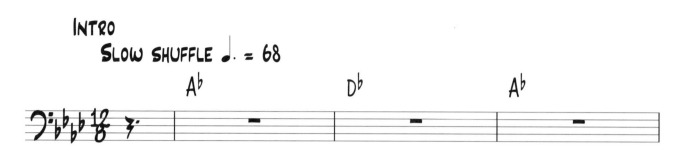

Texas Flood

Words and Music by Larry Davis and Joseph W. Scott

CD TRACK
◆ 8 Full Stereo Mix
◆ 16 Split Mix

𝄢 C Version

Intro
Slow shuffle ♩. = 68

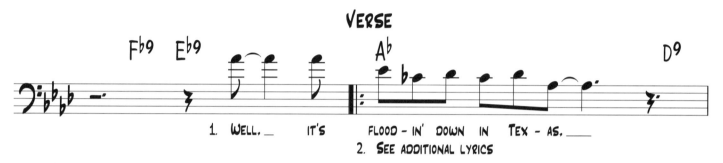

1. Well,___ it's flood-in' down in Tex-as,___
2. See additional lyrics

and all ___ the tel-e-phone lines _____ are down. Well,___ it's

flood-in' down ___ in Tex-as, and all ___ the tel-e-phone lines _____ are

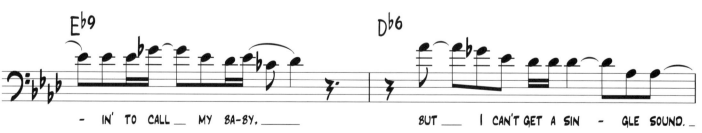

down. Well, I been try-

- in' to call ___ my ba-by, _____ but ___ I can't get a sin - gle sound. ___

Additional Lyrics

2. Well, dark clouds are rollin'.
   Man, I'm standin' out in the rain. Mm.
   Dark clouds are rollin'.
   Man, I'm standin' out in the rain.
   Well, flood waters keeps on rollin'.
   Man, it's about to drive me insane. Mm.

Presenting the Hal Leonard JAZZ PLAY-ALONG SERIES

For use with all B-flat, E-flat, Bass Clef and C instruments, the Jazz Play-Along® Series is the ultimate learning tool for all jazz musicians. With musician-friendly lead sheets, melody cues, and other split-track choices on the included CD, these first-of-a-kind packages help you master improvisation while playing some of the greatest tunes of all time. FOR STUDY, each tune includes a split track with: melody cue with proper style and inflection • professional rhythm tracks • choruses for soloing • removable bass part • removable piano part. FOR PERFORMANCE, each tune also has: an additional full stereo accompaniment track (no melody) • additional choruses for soloing.

1. DUKE ELLINGTON
00841644 .... $16.95

2. MILES DAVIS
00841645 .... $16.95

3. THE BLUES
00841646 .... $16.99

4. JAZZ BALLADS
00841691 .... $16.99

5. BEST OF BEBOP
00841689 .... $16.99

6. JAZZ CLASSICS WITH EASY CHANGES
00841690 .... $16.99

7. ESSENTIAL JAZZ STANDARDS
00843000 .... $16.99

8. ANTONIO CARLOS JOBIM AND THE ART OF THE BOSSA NOVA
00843001 .... $16.95

9. DIZZY GILLESPIE
00843002 .... $16.99

10. DISNEY CLASSICS
00843003 .... $16.99

11. RODGERS AND HART FAVORITES
00843004 .... $16.99

12. ESSENTIAL JAZZ CLASSICS
00843005 .... $16.99

13. JOHN COLTRANE
00843006 .... $16.95

14. IRVING BERLIN
00843007 .... $15.99

15. RODGERS & HAMMERSTEIN
00843008 .... $15.99

16. COLE PORTER
00843009 .... $15.95

17. COUNT BASIE
00843010 .... $16.95

18. HAROLD ARLEN
00843011 .... $15.95

19. COOL JAZZ
00843012 .... $15.95

20. CHRISTMAS CAROLS
00843080 .... $14.95

21. RODGERS AND HART CLASSICS
00843014 .... $14.95

22. WAYNE SHORTER
00843015 .... $16.95

23. LATIN JAZZ
00843016 .... $16.95

24. EARLY JAZZ STANDARDS
00843017 .... $14.95

25. CHRISTMAS JAZZ
00843018 .... $16.95

26. CHARLIE PARKER
00843019 .... $16.95

27. GREAT JAZZ STANDARDS
00843020 .... $15.99

28. BIG BAND ERA
00843021 .... $15.99

29. LENNON AND MCCARTNEY
00843022 .... $16.95

30. BLUES' BEST
00843023 .... $15.99

31. JAZZ IN THREE
00843024 .... $15.99

32. BEST OF SWING
00843025 .... $15.99

33. SONNY ROLLINS
00843029 .... $15.95

34. ALL TIME STANDARDS
00843030 .... $15.99

35. BLUESY JAZZ
00843031 .... $15.99

36. HORACE SILVER
00843032 .... $16.99

37. BILL EVANS
00843033 .... $16.95

38. YULETIDE JAZZ
00843034 .... $16.95

39. "ALL THE THINGS YOU ARE" & MORE JEROME KERN SONGS
00843035 .... $15.99

40. BOSSA NOVA
00843036 .... $15.99

41. CLASSIC DUKE ELLINGTON
00843037 .... $16.99

42. GERRY MULLIGAN FAVORITES
00843038 .... $16.99

43. GERRY MULLIGAN CLASSICS
00843039 .... $16.95

44. OLIVER NELSON
00843040 .... $16.95

45. JAZZ AT THE MOVIES
00843041 .... $15.99

46. BROADWAY JAZZ STANDARDS
00843042 .... $15.99

47. CLASSIC JAZZ BALLADS
00843043 .... $15.99

48. BEBOP CLASSICS
00843044 .... $16.99

49. MILES DAVIS STANDARDS
00843045 .... $16.95

50. GREAT JAZZ CLASSICS
00843046 .... $15.99

51. UP-TEMPO JAZZ
00843047 .... $15.99

52. STEVIE WONDER
00843048 .... $15.95

53. RHYTHM CHANGES
00843049 .... $15.99

54. **"MOONLIGHT IN VERMONT" AND OTHER GREAT STANDARDS**
00843050 ....$15.99

55. **BENNY GOLSON**
00843052 ....$15.95

56. **"GEORGIA ON MY MIND" & OTHER SONGS BY HOAGY CARMICHAEL**
00843056 ....$15.99

57. **VINCE GUARALDI**
00843057 ....$16.99

58. **MORE LENNON AND MCCARTNEY**
00843059 ....$15.99

59. **SOUL JAZZ**
00843060 ....$15.99

60. **DEXTER GORDON**
00843061 ....$15.95

61. **MONGO SANTAMARIA**
00843062 ....$15.95

62. **JAZZ-ROCK FUSION**
00843063 ....$14.95

63. **CLASSICAL JAZZ**
00843064 ....$14.95

64. **TV TUNES**
00843065 ....$14.95

65. **SMOOTH JAZZ**
00843066 ....$16.99

66. **A CHARLIE BROWN CHRISTMAS**
00843067 ....$16.99

67. **CHICK COREA**
00843068 ....$15.95

68. **CHARLES MINGUS**
00843069 ....$16.95

69. **CLASSIC JAZZ**
00843071 ....$15.99

70. **THE DOORS**
00843072 ....$14.95

71. **COLE PORTER CLASSICS**
00843073 ....$14.95

72. **CLASSIC JAZZ BALLADS**
00843074 ....$15.99

73. **JAZZ/BLUES**
00843075 ....$14.95

74. **BEST JAZZ CLASSICS**
00843076 ....$15.99

75. **PAUL DESMOND**
00843077 ....$14.95

76. **BROADWAY JAZZ BALLADS**
00843078 ....$15.99

77. **JAZZ ON BROADWAY**
00843079 ....$15.99

78. **STEELY DAN**
00843070 ....$14.99

79. **MILES DAVIS CLASSICS**
00843081 ....$15.99

80. **JIMI HENDRIX**
00843083 ....$15.99

81. **FRANK SINATRA – CLASSICS**
00843084 ....$15.99

82. **FRANK SINATRA – STANDARDS**
00843085 ....$15.99

83. **ANDREW LLOYD WEBBER**
00843104 ....$14.95

84. **BOSSA NOVA CLASSICS**
00843105 ....$14.95

85. **MOTOWN HITS**
00843109 ....$14.95

86. **BENNY GOODMAN**
00843110 ....$14.95

87. **DIXIELAND**
00843111 ....$14.95

88. **DUKE ELLINGTON FAVORITES**
00843112 ....$14.95

89. **IRVING BERLIN FAVORITES**
00843113 ....$14.95

90. **THELONIOUS MONK CLASSICS**
00841262 ....$16.99

91. **THELONIOUS MONK FAVORITES**
00841263 ....$16.99

92. **LEONARD BERNSTEIN**
00450134 ....$14.99

93. **DISNEY FAVORITES**
00843142 ....$14.99

94. **RAY**
00843143 ....$14.95

95. **JAZZ AT THE LOUNGE**
00843144 ....$14.99

96. **LATIN JAZZ STANDARDS**
00843145 ....$14.99

97. **MAYBE I'M AMAZED**
00843148 ....$14.99

98. **DAVE FRISHBERG**
00843149 ....$15.99

99. **SWINGING STANDARDS**
00843150 ....$14.99

100. **LOUIS ARMSTRONG**
00740423 ....$15.99

101. **BUD POWELL**
00843152 ....$14.99

102. **JAZZ POP**
00843153 ....$14.99

103. **ON GREEN DOLPHIN STREET & OTHER JAZZ CLASSICS**
00843154 ....$14.99

104. **ELTON JOHN**
00843155 ....$14.99

105. **SOULFUL JAZZ**
00843151 ....$14.99

106. **SLO' JAZZ**
00843117 ....$14.99

107. **MOTOWN CLASSICS**
00843116 ....$14.99

111. **COOL CHRISTMAS**
00843162 ....$15.99

HAL•LEONARD BLUES PLAY-ALONG

For use with all the C, B♭, Bass Clef and E♭ Instruments, the Hal Leonard Blues Play-Along Series is the ultimate jamming tool for all blues musicians.

With easy-to-read lead sheets, and other split-track choices on the included CD, these first-of-a-kind packages will bring your local blues jam right into your house! Each song on the CD includes two tracks: a full stereo mix, and a split track mix with removable guitar, bass, piano, and harp parts. The CD is playable on any CD player, and is also enhanced so Mac and PC users can adjust the recording to any tempo without changing the pitch!

1. Chicago Blues

All Your Love (I Miss Loving) • Easy Baby • I Ain't Got You • I'm Your Hoochie Coochie Man • Killing Floor • Mary Had a Little Lamb • Messin' with the Kid • Sweet Home Chicago.

00843106 Book/CD Pack $12.99

2. Texas Blues

Hide Away • If You Love Me Like You Say • Mojo Hand • Okie Dokie Stomp • Pride and Joy • Reconsider Baby • T-Bone Shuffle • The Things That I Used to Do.

00843107 Book/CD Pack $12.99

3. Slow Blues

Don't Throw Your Love on Me So Strong • Five Long Years • I Can't Quit You Baby • I Just Want to Make Love to You • The Sky Is Crying • (They Call It) Stormy Monday (Stormy Monday Blues) • Sweet Little Angel • Texas Flood.

00843108 Book/CD Pack $12.99

4. Shuffle Blues

Beautician Blues • Bright Lights, Big City • Further on up the Road • I'm Tore Down • Juke • Let Me Love You Baby • Look at Little Sister • Rock Me Baby.

00843171 Book/CD Pack $12.99

5. B.B. King

Everyday I Have the Blues • It's My Own Fault Darlin' • Just Like a Woman • Please Accept My Love • Sweet Sixteen • The Thrill Is Gone • Why I Sing the Blues • You Upset Me Baby.

00843172 Book/CD Pack $12.99

6. Jazz Blues

Birk's Works • Blues in the Closet • Cousin Mary • Freddie Freeloader • Now's the Time • Tenor Madness • Things Ain't What They Used to Be • Turnaround.

00843175 Book/CD Pack $12.99

7. Howlin' Wolf

Built for Comfort • Forty-Four • How Many More Years • Killing Floor • Moanin' at Midnight • Shake for Me • Sitting on Top of the World • Smokestack Lightning.

00843176 Book/CD Pack $12.99

8. Blues Classics

Baby, Please Don't Go • Boom Boom • Born Under a Bad Sign • Dust My Broom • How Long, How Long Blues • I Ain't Superstitious • It Hurts Me Too • My Babe.

00843177 Book/CD Pack $12.99

9. Albert Collins

Brick • Collins' Mix • Don't Lose Your Cool • Frost Bite • Frosty • I Ain't Drunk • Master Charge • Trash Talkin'.

00843178 Book/CD Pack $12.99

10. Uptempo Blues

Cross Road Blues (Crossroads) • Give Me Back My Wig • Got My Mo Jo Working • The House Is Rockin' • Paying the Cost to Be the Boss • Rollin' and Tumblin' • Turn on Your Love Light • You Can't Judge a Book by the Cover.

00843179 Book/CD Pack $12.99